ANIMAL VS ANIMAL

WHO'S THE

BENDIEST?

BY EMILIE DUFRESNE

BookLife
PUBLISHING

©2019
BookLife Publishing
King's Lynn
Norfolk PE30 4LS

All rights reserved.
Printed in Malaysia.

A catalogue record for this
book is available from the
British Library.

ISBN: 978-1-78637-523-0

Written by:
Emilie Dufresne

Edited by:
Holly Duhig

Designed by:
Danielle Rippengill

All facts, statistics, web addresses and URLs in this book were verified as valid and accurate at time of writing.
No responsibility for any changes to external websites or references can be accepted by either the author or publisher.

IMAGE CREDITS

All images are courtesy of Shutterstock.com, unless otherwise specified. With thanks to Getty Images, Thinkstock Photo and iStockphoto.
Cover – Ovocheva, Stepova Oksana, Abscent. Images used on every page – Ovocheva, Stepova Oksana. 5 – ONYXprj, Abscent. 6&7 – Guingm.
8 – EB Adventure Photography. 9 – Stan Shebs [GFDL (http://www.gnu.org/copyleft/fdl.html), CC BY-SA 3.0 (https://creativecommons.org/licenses/by-sa/3.0) or CC BY-SA 2.5 (https://creativecommons.org/licenses/by-sa/2.5)], from Wikimedia Commons. 8&9 – Guingm. 10&11 – Abscent.
12 – otsphoto. 13 – turtix. 12&13 – Guingm. 14&15 – ArchOnez, Abscent. 16 – Vladimir Wrangel. 17 – Irina Kozorog. 16&17 – Guingm. 18&19 – Abscent.
20&21 – amiloslava. 22 – Guingm. 23 – Abscent.

CONTENTS

Words that look like this can be found in the glossary on page 24.

THE GREAT AND SMALL GAMES

Roll Up! Roll Up!

It's the Great and Small Games!
See nature's bendiest and most flexible creatures in action!

Today's events:
The Knot Tie!
The Tunnel Turn!
The Squish-a-Thon!

These events will surely decide once and for all:
Who's the Bendiest?

Gather round, and feast your eyes,
on agile animals that are SURE to SURPRISE,
with bendy backs and flexible frames,
who **is going to win** these games?
So WITHOUT HESITATION, let's look and see,
Who will have the **victory?**

THE CONTENDERS

Let's find out some facts and figures about today's contenders!

Rat
The Big Squeeze

Size: 12 centimetres (cm) long

Lives: Worldwide

Stretch Stats: Wriggling through holes the size of its head

Cat
The Flexi-Feline

Size: 45 cm long

Lives: Worldwide

Stretch Stats: Can rotate its body in two different directions whilst in the air

Ferret
The Rotating Rodent

Size: Over 60 cm long including tail

Lives: Europe, Asia, Africa and North America

Stretch Stats: Super stretchy spine

Octopus
The Boneless Blob

Size: Around 1 metre (m)

Lives: Tropical and **temperate** oceans

Stretch Stats:
Can squeeze through tiny gaps

Hagfish
Slip 'n' Slide

Size: Over 1 m long

Lives: Cold waters across the world

Stretch Stats:
No backbone

Californian Sea Lion
Roly Poly Pup

Size: Up to 2.5 m long

Lives: North America

Stretch Stats:
Very flexible neck

SEA LION VS

Rrrrrrround Onnnne!

ARP! ARP!

This sea lion is super stretchy and bendy. With a head that can be bent all the way back so that he can look behind him, you would think these animals didn't have a neck!

Nickname:
Roly Poly Pup

Flexi-Fact: Being able to bend their necks all the way back means that sea lions can make sharp turns in the water.

HAGFISH

This bendy bottom-feeder lives in the depths of the ocean and feeds on rotting **carcasses**. But he always makes time to stretch, and is one of the most flexible animals in the world.

Nickname:
Slip 'n' Slide

Flexi-Fact: With a skull but no spine, hagfish can twist and turn into all sorts of shapes!

Hagfish have very loose skin that helps them to bend into any shape without tearing.

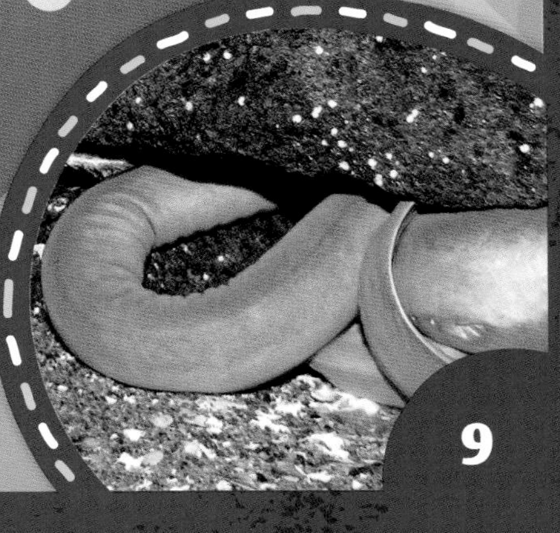

LET'S TWIST

THE KNOT TIE

Contenders, to test your flexibility we will be doing the knot tie! Whoever can tie themselves into a knot first will be the winner. The sea lion is trying his best to twist his body around, but bending his neck is the best he can do.

Sea lions also have very flexible hips that let them move on land very easily by **rotating** their flippers under their body.

Let's see how the hagfish is getting on. The hagfish has twisted his body into a knot and seems to be covered in sticky slime...

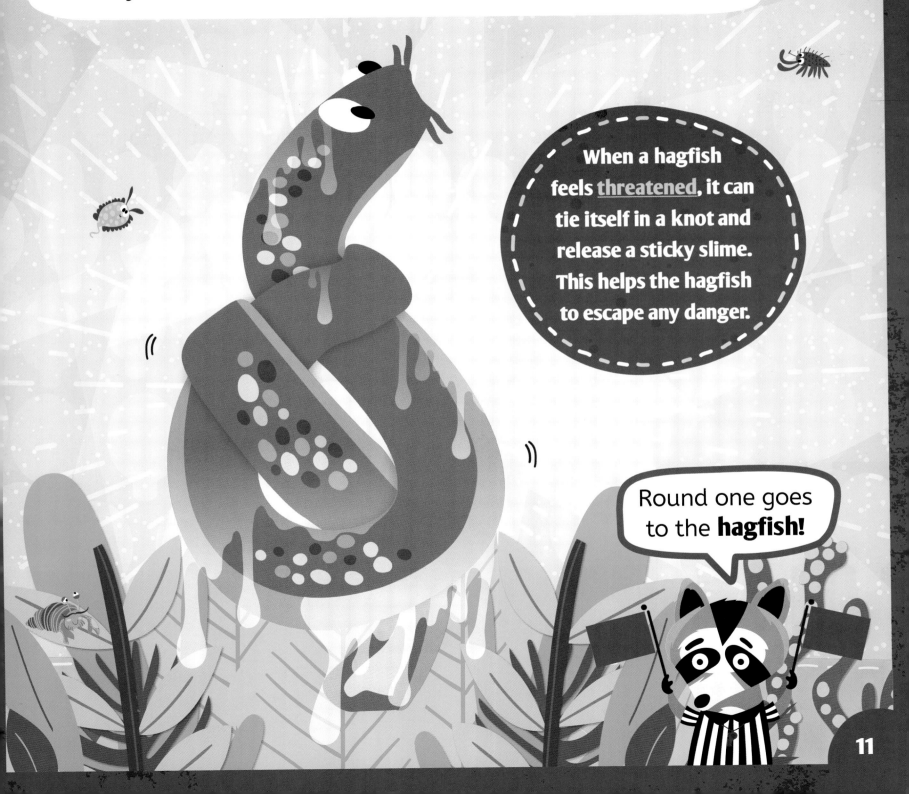

When a hagfish feels <u>threatened</u>, it can tie itself in a knot and release a sticky slime. This helps the hagfish to escape any danger.

Round one goes to the **hagfish!**

FERRET VS

Rrrrrrround Twoooo!

DOOK! DOOK!

This wriggly weasel can worm his way through any gap. Ferrets have very long spines which help them turn in tight spaces.

Nickname:
The Rotating Rodent

Flexi-Fact: Humans have 33 **vertebrae** (say: ver-ter-bray) in their spine, whilst ferrets have 46. That's a lot more places to bend!

CAT

Our feline friend has a fiercely flexible trick up his sleeve. If he falls from a height, he can rotate his body really quickly and always land on his feet!

Nickname:
The Flexi-Feline

Flexi-Fact: A cat uses its whiskers to know whether it can fit into a space or not!

Cats have flexible spines; this helps them perform amazing tricks such as jumping nine times their height!

PURRR!

THE TUNNEL TURN

Each contender has a tunnel not much wider than they are. They must enter the tunnel, turn around and come back out. The first animal out of the tunnel is the winner!

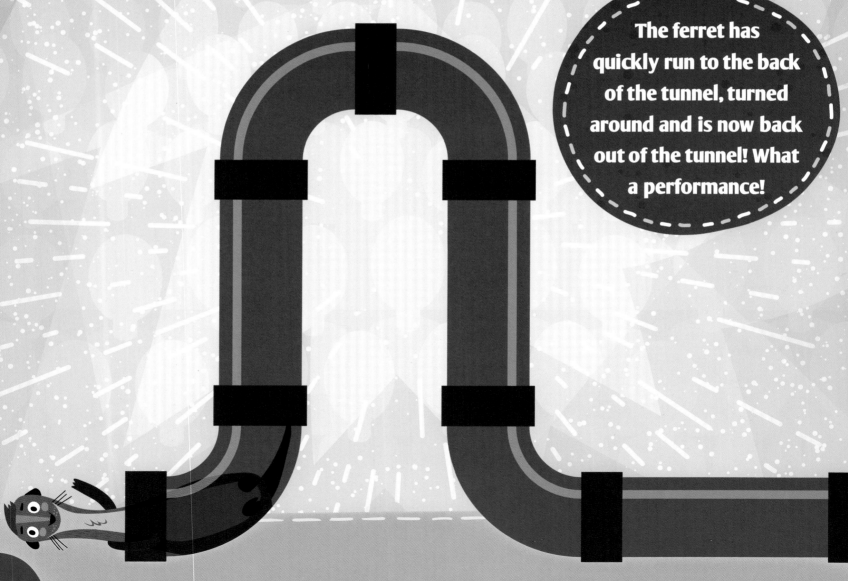

The ferret has quickly run to the back of the tunnel, turned around and is now back out of the tunnel! What a performance!

The cat is slowly making his way through the tunnel. It will take him a while to turn in this tight space, but he will get out eventually. Unfortunately, it's not quick enough to beat the Rotating Rodent!

Round two goes to the **ferret!**

Cats are usually ambush <u>predators</u>. This means that they hide in small spaces and suddenly jump out at their <u>prey</u>.

OCTOPUS

Rrrrrrround Threee!

With amazing **camouflage** and the ability to ward off predators with a squirt of ink, the Boneless Blob is ready to squeeze himself into first place.

Nickname:
The Boneless Blob

Flexi-Fact:
Octopuses can squeeze their **bulbous** heads through any gap that their beaks can fit through.

VS RAT

A mischievous, yet **malleable** creature, this contender is ready for the big squeeze! With razor-sharp teeth that can chew through metal, this rat is not messing around.

Nickname:
The Big Squeeze

Flexi-Fact:
Rats have folding rib cages that help them squeeze through holes as small as 2.5 cm wide!

The outer layer of a rat's tooth is harder than platinum.

NIBBLE! NIBBLE!

THE SQUISH-A-THON

Both contenders will have to twist and bend their bodies into weird and wonderful positions to try to get out of the tiny hole they are faced with.

When moving through a small gap, an octopus will move legs first and pull his head out last.

The rat is squishing himself through the tiny hole, but he has got stuck halfway through and is now trying to gnaw his way out! Wait a second, the octopus is already out!

Round three goes to the **octopus!**

HALL OF FAME

Great Horned Owl
This creature can turn its head up to 270 degrees.

Lives: North and South America

Eats: Small animals such mice and voles

Size: 63 cm tall, 1.5 m **wingspan**

Worm
Having no skeleton lets this worm wriggle his way through life.

Lives: Europe, North America and western Asia

Eats: Soil, leaves and poo

Size: Up to 35 cm long

Elephant
Elephant trunks are very flexible and have strong muscles.

Lives: South Asia, Southeast Asia and sub-Saharan Africa

Eats: Trees, leaves and plants

Size: Over 3 m tall

Spider Monkey
These monkeys have strong, flexible tails that help them climb.

Lives: Central and South America

Eats: Nuts, fruit, eggs and spiders

Size: 66 cm long

QUIZ AND...

We've seen the creatures stretch and twist,
It's now time to see who's cleverest!

Questions

1. How big must a hole be for an octopus to squeeze through it?

2. What helps sea lions make tight turns in the water?

3. What can a hagfish produce when it feels threatened?

4. How many vertebrae does a ferret have?

5. What part of its body does a cat use to know whether or not it can fit into a space?

6. What hard material can rats chew through?

Answers: 1. As big as its beak 2. Being able to bend their neck all the way back 3. Slime 4. 46 5. Its whiskers 6. Metal

ACTIVITY

How flexible are you? Try some of these moves to see how flexible you are! Can you pull funny faces? For example, can you raise one eyebrow while pulling the other one down? Now try these stretches!

Bend over forwards and keep your knees straight. How close can you get your hands to the ground?

Sit on the ground with your back straight. How far apart can you stretch your legs?

GLOSSARY

bulbous	big and round
camouflage	traits that allow an animal to hide itself in a habitat
carcasses	the bodies of dead animals
malleable	can be made to change shape
predators	animals that eat other animals for food
prey	animals that are eaten by other animals for food
rotating	turning in a circle around a fixed point
temperate	a place or area that is usually a mild temperature
threatened	to feel frightened or scared of something
vertebrae	the small bones that make up the spine
wingspan	the distance the between the tips of a bird's wings

INDEX

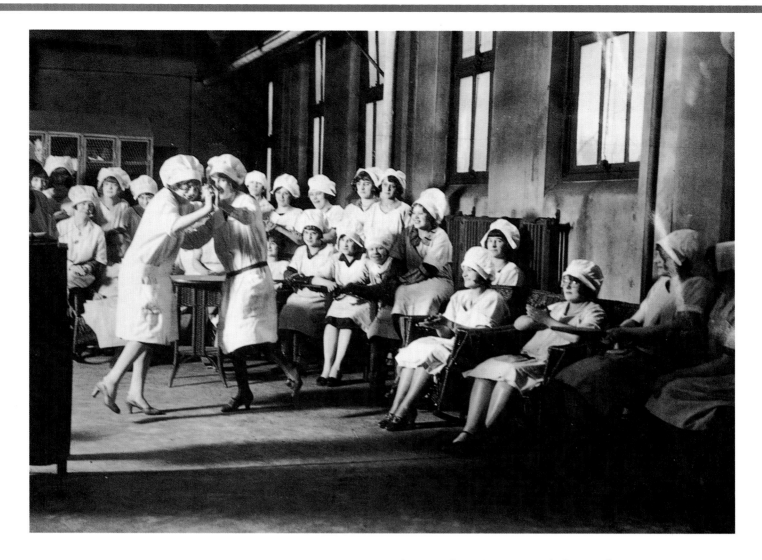

▲ The Charleston originated amongst black dock workers in South Carolina, and quickly became popular worldwide. These nurses from the 1920s are performing the rapid kicking step that was typical of the dance.

Another popular black dance was called the Juba, which was also said to ·have come from Africa. In America it was known as the 'patting Juba', as there was much stamping, clapping, slapping and patting of arms, chest and thighs. In this dance, a woman would advance into the centre of a circle of dancers. She would choose a male rival and they would both compete by twisting and jerking their bodies until one dancer gave up. The rest of the dancers kept time by clapping, stamping and slapping their thighs.

The European settlers soon began to imitate the slaves' dances. In the twentieth century, dances such as the Charleston became popular. This was originally a round dance performed by dock workers in Charleston, South Carolina. In the 1920s it became a fast step, in which the feet were kicked forwards and backwards. The Black Bottom consisted of stamping and shuffling the feet and swaying the knees.

17

New Orleans still has many festivals and dance traditions that show the influence of black culture. One such dance is John Canoe, which occurs today at the time of Mardi Gras. Groups of specially costumed dancers parade through the streets carrying wooden swords, followed by a group of women. The women divide themselves into rival groups, each led by a 'queen'. They call themselves the 'reds' and 'blues' because of the colours of the clothes they wear. The men wear masks in the shape of houses on their heads.

▲ The brightly coloured costume of this Mexican dancer is a traditional Aztec design, inspired by the myths and legends about the Quetzal bird.

In the Mexican Volodores dance, the ▶ dancers throw themselves from a pole and fly like birds, attached with ropes.

No one knows for certain the origin of the dance, but it may have been performed to honour John Connay, who was famous in New Orleans in the early eighteenth century.

Over 500 years ago, the Aztec people of Mexico had many varied and complex dances. When the Spanish explorers arrived in the fifteenth century and conquered the Aztec empire, many of their customs and dances were forbidden and they were forced to adopt Christian beliefs. The people of Mexico have not forgotten their ancient customs, however, and today some of their dances are similar to those of Aztec times. The Volodores, or flying pole dance, is the most thrilling and beautiful of all. The Volodores was originally an Aztec dance to honour the wind, but nowadays it is performed on saints' days and for tourists. A tall, straight tree trunk is set up in the middle of a square, with a small revolving platform at the top. Four flyers and a musician climb the pole. After a ceremony performed by the musician on the platform, the flyers throw themselves from the top of the pole, with ropes attached around their waists. As the ropes unwind they fly like birds, rotating around the pole thirteen times until they reach the ground. As they fly, the music increases in intensity. The flyers dress as birds – some wear a crest of feathers on their heads, and feathers on their backs to look like wings.

Central and South America

In the seventeenth and eighteenth centuries, many people were taken from Africa and transported by ship across the Atlantic Ocean to America. On the boats, they were forced to dance as a way of keeping healthy. They were used as slaves on the plantations in the Caribbean islands of Haiti, Trinidad, Jamaica and Cuba. Life here was very hard, and dancing was a way in which the slaves could remember their traditions and have some fun. The Calenda was a popular African dance, from the coast of Guinea. In the Calenda, the dancers were arranged in two lines facing each other, the men dancing on one side and the women on the other. The dancers jumped, turned and moved backwards and forwards to the music of singing, clapping and drums. In the Chica dance, a woman, holding the ends of a handkerchief or the sides of her skirt, would rotate her hips while keeping the upper part of her body almost still. The Chica was danced all over the Caribbean, and was even danced by nuns at Christmas.

There were many religious dances in

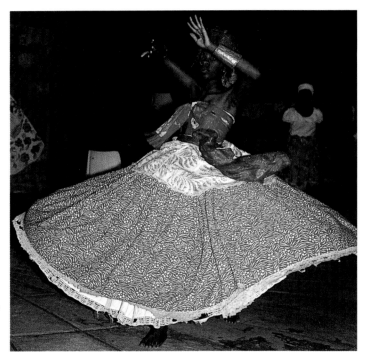

the Caribbean, but the most famous of all is voodoo dancing. Voodoo is a mixture of African beliefs and Catholicism, and it was extremely popular on the island of Haiti. In a voodoo ceremony, a person becomes possessed by a god, known as a loa. Voodoo dancing consists of violent shaking of the shoulders and head, until finally the dancer may collapse. The music is created by sacred drums, rattles,

◀ A spiritual priestess of the Candomblé religion, dancing to the god Yansã, in Brazil. The Candomblé is a religion with direct African influences.

Children dancing ▶ in Cuba. They are shaking their shoulders and rotating their hips – movements which originated in African dance traditions.

bamboo tubes and an iron plate called an ogan, which is struck with another piece of metal. The dances vary, depending on which god possesses the person. These sacred ceremonial dances are rarely seen even today – traditionally they were conducted in secret, and they are not performed for tourists.

▲ Many lively, flamboyant dances are performed as entertainments in bars and theatres. These dancers are performing at the Tropicana club in Havana, Cuba.

Dancers performing the Samba, a fast-moving ▶ dance, at a carnival in Brazil.

Some Caribbean dances were taken to South America when Caribbean people started to migrate there, and these became mixed with local dances. One of the most interesting is the Tango from Argentina. The Tango is believed to have originated from a mixture of three different dances – the Tangano from Africa, the Habanera from Cuba and the Milonga from Argentina. The Tango was a flamboyant dance that became popular in the bars of the capital of Argentina, Buenos Aires. It then became extremely fashionable in Paris and other parts of Europe in the 1920s, where it developed into a more leisurely dance with a cat-like glide. This new form of the Tango spread around the world, and is still danced today, especially in Argentina.

▲ Bolivian folk dancers performing
a traditional dance at a celebration
near Lake Titicaca.

In Argentina today there is a
mixture of 'cowboy' dances, European
aristocratic dances and rural folk dances.
El Carnavalito is danced in north-west
Argentina, by people in both the poorer
rural areas and in dance halls and
ballrooms in the towns. It is most lively
in the mountainous areas of Jujuy and
Salta, where at fiesta time you can hear
the beat of drums as circles of men and
women – some with babies on their
backs – dance around groups of standing
musicians. They move in a chain or a
circle. The leader carries a handkerchief
or a ribboned stick, and sometimes
shouts in a high, hoarse voice. In this
form, El Carnavalito may last for hours.

Central and South America is a
region with many ancient traditions, and
a mixture of many different cultures.
Dance traditions in this area show the
influence of all these cultures.

▲ A Peruvian chain
dance, performed in
traditional costume.

24

Many of the dances of Central and ▶
South America have been influenced
by Spanish and Portuguese traditions.
This Peruvian folk dance is based on
flamenco, but is performed at a very
rapid pace.

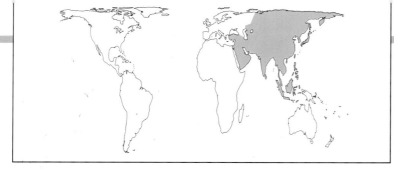

Asia

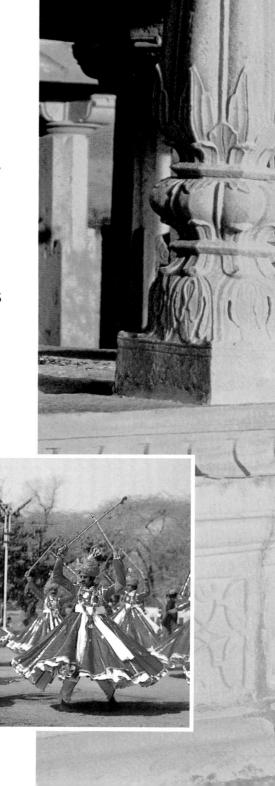

Dance traditions in Asia are very varied and lively. India has been the main influence on dancing styles in this area. Although many Indian dances are concerned with representing, imitating or worshipping the gods, some are purely for entertainment and fun.

Bharata Natyam is an important dance that is usually performed by a woman. The dancer wears tiny bells on her feet as she moves. She sings a series of songs, known as padas, in the middle of the performance, and acts out the words in detail with her hands. The palms of the dancer's hands, the soles of her feet and a large, round circle between her eyebrows are stained bright red with a special powder called temple powder. The performance ends with a Tillana dance. This consists of swift, lively bends and dips. The Tillanas tell no story – they simply convey happiness and joy.

Main picture: In India, women performing traditional dances often wear tiny bells on their ankles, which jingle as they move.

Dancers in Barmer, India, ▶ **dressed as bridegrooms for a festival.**

In Myanmar (Burma), dance traditions are also very lively. It is said that you cannot dance if you are sad, and the dancers smile throughout the performances, sometimes bursting out laughing. Normally, the dancer starts in a crouching position and begins by bowing, with his or her fingertips placed in front of the face. The hands twist and weave in alternating circles. The dancer sings a short phrase, and the drums beat the rhythm. Then, as the entire orchestra repeats the melody, the dancer leaps into the air with the arms twisting and curling. He or she then squats again and, with the knees bent, whirls around on one foot with the other leg extended. Finally, the dancer runs towards the spectators, pauses, claps three times and crosses his or her wrists, with the hands pointing downwards.

The dance traditions in Thailand and Cambodia are very similar to those of Myanmar. Movements are stylized and graceful, and different gestures can express emotions such as love, hate, anger and happiness.

Stylized hand movements are common features of Asian dance traditions, as in this Sri Lankan dance. ▶

In Japan, dance is also very controlled and stylized. Every movement or twist of the hand has some significance, and the dances tell historical stories and myths.

Although the Japanese have many beautiful and ancient theatrical traditions, they have also retained their folk dances, known as odori. The most famous and mysterious is the Bon dance. The Japanese believe that at certain points in the year the spirits of the dead come back to visit the living, and that they should be welcomed with singing and dancing. The dancers form a great circle, which revolves slowly, then quickly, then slowly again. They wave their arms to show emotions and worship. The figures glide around in the moonlight, their long sleeves waving like wings. Their steps are muffled and their songs are mixed with occasional soft clapping.

The Chinese Opera moves from smooth, gliding movements to whirling costumes and clashing spears. All the performances of the Cantonese or Beijing Operas tell stories or ancient legends, and there are pauses for high-pitched singing.

◀ A boy performing a bird dance in Kyoto, Japan. Japanese dances are often very stylized and graceful.

Inset picture: Barong dancers in Bali. Barong dances are performed by villages where bad spirits are believed to have settled. The dance re-enacts a battle between a protective lion figure, Barong, and an evil witch, Rangda.

Chinese lion and dragon dances are also very exciting to watch. Lion dances are always performed at Chinese New Year, and sometimes on special occasions such as the birthday of a god. The lion mask has a large head with long eyelashes, and a big mouth which can open and shut. Two people usually move the lion – one at the front, who moves the mouth and eyes, and the other at the back, who wriggles the lion's bottom and wags its tail. A drummer and several musicians follow the lion as it dances from place to place in time with the drum. The lion might stop outside a temple or restaurant to jump up and

catch a lettuce and a red packet hanging from a stick. Once the lion has caught the lettuce, it shreds it up and spits it all over the floor. It keeps the red packet, which has 'lucky' money inside. The lion's visit is seen as a way of blessing the place and bringing good luck and prosperity.

Although dance is closely linked to the theatre and the royal courts in Asia, there are also many local dances for healing the sick. In Sarawak in Malaysia, if a person is ill the medicine man does a frenzied dance. With a sword in his hand, he acts out a battle against the spirits who cause the illness. The Kayan of Sarawak perform a dance to help pregnant women give birth. The dancer is usually a female friend or relative of the woman in labour, and during her dance she dresses up a bundle of cloth to represent an infant. Amongst the Ifugao tribe in the Philippines, dancing is also considered to be a form of medicine. If all other treatments fail, a dance is believed to be the best cure for an illness.

Sri Lankan devil dancing can be performed whenever a person is sick, a woman is pregnant, whenever misfortune hits, or when good luck is needed. The dance usually takes place outside the house of the person concerned, in front of a specially built shrine. Although all the dancers are male, they dress as women, with red cloths on their heads and enormous bells on their ankles. The chief dancer becomes Vesamuni, the king of the demons. The dancers leap and swirl until about 4 a.m., when they put on masks and represent demons. The demon that has caused the sickness explains itself, and the patient is supposed to recover.

In Myanmar, spirit dances known as Nat Pwe are frequently held at New Year celebrations during the time of the April full moon. They are similar to the Sri Lankan devil dances, but are done to appease the spirits, known as nats. The dancers turn and spin, with one hand extended at the front and the other hand flung backwards, and work themselves into a trance.

Trance dances also take place on the islands of Indonesia. On Sumatra they are called Sanghyang. The most amazing is the fire dancing at Kayukapas. Two girls go into a trance with their eyes closed, and suddenly leap on to the shoulders of two men sitting near the orchestra. These men stand up and begin to dance, with the girls on their shoulders. The girls do back-bends and cling to the men's shoulders with only their toes. A fire of dried coconut shells is built, and the girls jump into it. They stamp and kick until the fire goes out. These girls are never burnt, and their costumes never catch fire. Sometimes they dance all night without tiring, and in the morning they cannot remember what they have done.

▲ In Indonesia, trance dancers like these two girls are able to perform feats of great daring, such as fire-walking.

Cambodian dance

It takes dancers many years of training to make their hands and wrists supple enough to do the gestures of Cambodian classical dance, but you can try to do some of the basic movements.

1. The sampieh, or salute of respect, is always done at the beginning or interval of a dance. Stand upright, touch your knees, then lift your hands up until they are at chest level. Place your palms together with your fingers curved back and your thumbs out, then raise them to your forehead.

◄ **The salute of respect is common to many traditional Asian dances, such as this one from Thailand.**

2. Stretch our your thumb and index finger until they almost touch in a point, and curl your other fingers backwards. This is the most common gesture of offering. You can indicate a smile by drawing your thumb and index finger across your mouth. You can show that you are crying by moving these fingers across your eyes.

◄ Traditional dancers in Cambodia train for many years. Here you can see the position in which the feet are held while dancing.

3. To walk, bend your knees, and put your heels together but your toes out. Hold your hands with the thumb and index fingers stretched out, as in Point 2, and sway back and forth a little. Place the heel of your right foot at the toe of your left foot, then the heel of your left foot at the toe of your right foot, and continue walking like this.

4. Rub the back of your ear to show that you are angry.

5. Cross your hands with all your fingers together, and gently pat your chest. You are now showing happiness or contentment.

6. Rub the palms of your hands together in a slow, circular motion to show greed or desire.

◄ This dancer in Thailand is using stylized movements to express feelings and ideas. The position of her hands features in the dance traditions of many Asian countries.

33

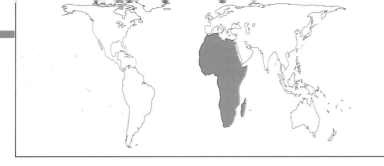

Africa

Many African dances take place at fixed times in the year as part of rituals. Sometimes there is a long gap between dances (as long as twenty years), but other dances are more frequent and regular. In some places, body movements are very important, and people are valued by the way they walk or stand. The Ngoni of Malawi say that dance is a force that reveals a person's character and birthright.

The Zulu of South Africa have many different dances for different occasions. The Ndlamu dance is particularly popular. Young men form a single or double line. Some raise their legs forwards and kick before bringing their foot down, while others raise the knee and then swing the leg backwards with a piston action before stamping. Sometimes the dancers throw themselves on the ground at the final moment of the dance. This dance is performed mainly for pleasure, and is most spectacular when performed with a hundred or more dancers.

In the nineteenth century, whole regiments of Zulu soldiers would dance the Ngama Makosi, or royal dance, in front of their chiefs on special occasions. The men danced barefoot, giving the performances a muffled sound. Because there were so many dancers,

Step dances, as performed by this dancer in ▶ Johannesburg, are very popular amongst the Zulu people of South Africa.

34

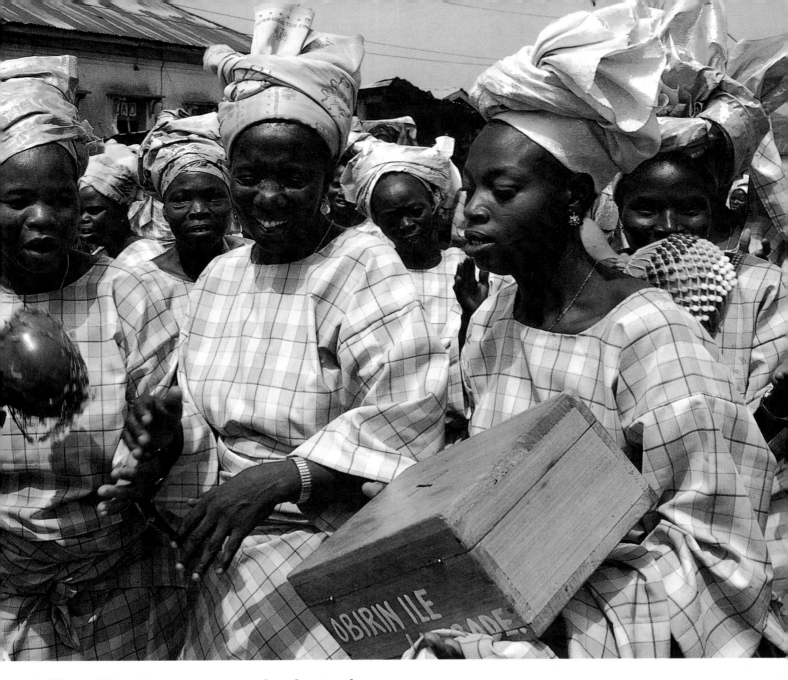

▲ These Nigerian women are dancing to the
accompaniment of traditional percussion instruments.

the Zulu used to say that they sounded
like the waves of the sea breaking along
the shore.

Zulu men also do a step dance
called Isicathulo, or boot dance. Originally
this was performed by Zulu pupils at
mission schools, where the Christian
authorities banned other local dances. It
became popular for the pupils to wear

shoes and boots, which made the dance
much noisier. Many years later, Zulu
dock workers in Durban, South Africa,
were given Wellington boots to protect
their feet while they handled cargoes of
chemical fertilizers. They began to use
the boots in their dances, slapping them
with their hands and clapping them
together with their feet.

In Kenya and Tanzania, men also dance in groups or teams. Dance societies are called Beni, after the English word 'band', and a dance team is called a ngoma. These teams used to wear European-style military uniforms, and paraded up and down like a military drill. The team leader, known as the king, wore a cap of rank, shoulder badges, and a row of fountain pens in his breast pocket. He would march up and down in front of his men. The other dancers dressed in a uniform of white shorts and a shirt, and a band played bugles, pipes and drums, like a British brass band. Some of the accompanying songs reflected African opposition to colonial rule, and the dance was seen as a form of protest.

The Beni dances were always performed by men, but there was a similar dance for women called Lelemana. The women paraded in the streets, wearing the costumes of the

Many traditional African dances are ▶ accompanied by percussion instruments. While these Ninga drummers from Burundi beat out a rhythm, a dancer performs outstanding feats of athletic movement.

British air force, army and navy. Some women carried wooden guns. Such dances became important when the British governed Kenya, but nowadays they are not performed so frequently.

Dance competitions are important in Africa. Amongst the Kerebe of Tanzania, the local people used to form dance associations, and used magic, sorcery and acts of daring to divert attention away from their rivals. In the past, the team with the largest audience would win the contest. When dancing in this region was stopped by colonialism, popular interest shifted to football, which had the same competitive spirit.

The Wodaabe of Niger have dancing competitions in which the women decide which man is the most beautiful. The first dance of the competition is called the Yake. The men take many hours to prepare themselves for this. They lighten their faces with a yellow powder, blacken their lips to

◀ Nowadays, many African dances, like dances all over the world, are frequently performed for tourists. This dance group is in the middle of a performance at a club in Kenya.

highlight the whiteness of their teeth, and outline their eyes to make them stand out. The Yake is danced slowly with the knees bent, one foot over the other and the hands clapping. The dancers stand shoulder to shoulder, and quiver forward on tiptoe to make themselves look taller. Sometimes they stamp and jump with great energy. Their facial expressions are designed to show their charm and personality. The elders dash up and down the line, mocking and criticizing the men in an effort to make them work harder. The women circle round the group, clapping their hands.

The second stage of the contest is called the Geerewol, where the most beautiful men are selected. The men line up before the audience, shouting haunting chants, and do frenzied jumping and stamping steps for up to two hours. Three unmarried women are brought out to judge the competition. After they have decided, the women indicate their favourites with graceful swings of their arms.

◄ **Courtship dances are performed by many African peoples. This Lusaka woman from Zambia is taking part in a dancing competition with a male dancer, as part of a courtship ceremony.**

The Hausa of Nigeria also hold dancing competitions, but for very different reasons. Dance is linked to the spirits, known as bori, and each town has its own bori cult. These bori spirits have a passion for dancing, and each one has its own dancing rhythm and character, such as a prince, a slave or an old woman. To attract certain spirits to a local market, the drummers beat out rhythms which tempt the spirits to possess them. If the dancing attracts a large audience, it is believed that the town will become richer.

Amongst the Venda of South Africa, dances are associated with education.

Girls learn a series of dances with contrasting styles to prepare them for motherhood. One dance, the Damba, marks a girl's transformation to adulthood. The Tshikana is the most important Venda dance and is connected with ancestor worship. It is said to make sick people feel better.

The Baka of Cameroon also have special dances which are performed to cure the sick. The fire dance takes place at night, and the whole village is involved. The sick person sits or lies down by the fire and watches the movements. There is much singing, shaking, clapping and drumming. The dancers may approach the sick person to see how he or she is and to share a joke. An elder will then approach the sick person and place a hot sword on him or her as a cure.

Masai dancers from ▶ Kenya, performing a traditional group dance for tourists.

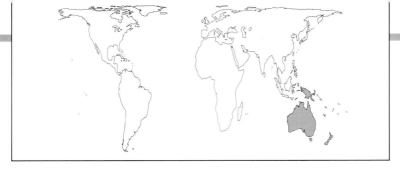

The Pacific

Dance has a special place in Pacific life. It is seen as a way of entertaining and having fun, and it can also communicate serious messages. Before writing came to the Pacific, the history of a village was passed on in songs, stories and dance. Dancing is still a way in which children are taught to remember their past. Certain Maori dances in New Zealand, for example, help to explain Maori history by imitating the paddling of the first canoes to set out from Polynesia to New Zealand.

On the islands of Samoa, Tonga, Tahiti and Hawaii, people still keep alive their dance, music and singing traditions. Dancing is closely linked to song. Dancers first learn a song, then they sing this while they learn the dance movements. Most of the dances are linked to ancient tales and legends. The focus of movement is always on the upper body, and the arms and hands move the most and tell the stories. In Tahiti the word for dance is 'aparima', which translates as 'hand mime'.

In Tonga, some dances are done sitting down. Otuhaka and Faha'iula are two such dances and are performed by women of high rank for the entertainment of the court, and to show the grace of female arms and hands. Drum beats, chanting and clapping accompany the women's movements.

Children on the ▶ island of Tonga, using their hands to perform a seated dance.

◄ These fire dancers from Samoa twirl torches fuelled by diesel oil. Fire dances are very dangerous, and only experienced dancers may take part.

◄ These dancers in Hawaii have sewn large leaves together to make costumes. They are performing the hula, a dance which originally was performed to honour the gods or to praise chiefs and kings. Nowadays, hulas tell stories or describe places through the dancers' movements.

In the Pacific region, dancers often wear dance costumes made out of leaves. The leaves are strung together like a necklace, then sewn into skirts. Cotton tunics are worn underneath.

In the Samoan Taualuga dance, a solo dancer performs small, slow movements in the centre of the stage and is surrounded by other people dancing vigorously. The solo dancer is called Ali'i, or chief, and is of high rank, whereas the dancers at the sides are called Tulafala. They are supposed to be noisy and unpredictable, and to come from the lower ranks of Samoan society.

Energetic dances are also performed to show physical fitness, balance and co-ordination. The Sasa is a group-action dance from Samoa, which is done to the sounds of a furiously beaten drum. It involves very quick steps, fast running in which the heels touch the buttocks, and sudden changes in direction. A comedian or clown dances at the side of the group. He is allowed to take centre stage from time to time and often his dance can be quite outrageous.

Tonga's most important formal dance is called the Lakalaka and involves over 100 dancers. The spectators decorate their favourite dancers with tokens of affection, such as cloth or money. Coconut oil is rubbed on to the dancers' bodies before the dance, so that the gifts can stick to them. In some places it is not unusual to see dancers covered from head to foot with dollar bills and other presents.

There are many celebrations and dancing competitions throughout the year on the Polynesian islands. Nowadays, dances are also performed to entertain tourists.

On the large island of Papua New Guinea, the dance traditions are very different. In the Highland areas the performers are mainly groups of men, who use the occasion to show off their spectacular decoration. Dances occur at the Pig Festivals amongst the Wahgi and Melpa peoples. The aim of these dances is to dazzle rivals with the display. Melpa men spend much time preparing themselves for a dance. They put on feathers, shells, leaves and grasses, face paint, charcoal, wigs, belts and aprons. The dancing can go on for hours at a time, and their wives bring them water and small pieces of food to keep them going. In the Mor dance, each group of men forms a single line or extended horseshoe shape and faces a rival group.

Drums and whistles accompany the dancing, and the men sing. As the rhythm gets faster, the lines of dancers pivot on their toes, their feathered head-dresses swinging back and forth.

Wahgi men also dance in a line form at the Pig Festivals. Their dancing is like a jogging movement, and as the jingling of their shell belts increases they all break into a long 'Ooooo' chant. The dancers turn to face each other with their backs to the audience, and they may all begin to bang their drums. They alternate between singing and drumming, turning inwards and outwards for an hour or so. The most spectacular event is at the end of the Pig Festival. The men charge on to the dance ground, circle the sacred house at the centre and climb on to the platform on the roof. Great quantities of pigs are killed and eaten in front of the spectators.

**Body decoration, ►
especially face
painting, is common in
the traditional dances
of the Highlands of
Papua New Guinea,
such as this Huli sing-
sing dance.**

The Australian Aborigines have many dances linked to their ancient beliefs and ceremonies. For the Warlpiri, women's dances are always performed as part of rituals, and act out Dreamtime events. Dreamtime is believed to be the beginning of the world, when the Aborigines' ancestors moved about, forming landscapes and creating animals, plants and people. The Warlpiri dances teach young women about this

▲ Aboriginal dances are used to pass traditional beliefs, myths and legends from generation to generation.

time and remind them of the source of power in their universe. Through these dances they are taught many important things about their culture, such as local history and when, where and how to find food and water.

▲ The dance traditions of the Pacific area are kept alive by regular dance competitions and festivals. These Maori women are performing at a festival in Rarotonga.

Other dances are linked to fertility or rain rituals. In north-west Australia, the Aborigines circle around a magic stone which is thought to bring rain. The men of the Watchandi tribe in Western Australia perform a fertility ritual during the Spring Festival. At night, after the women and children leave, the men dance alone around a hole dug in the ground, accompanied by cries and songs. After a long time, as the dance speeds up, they plunge their spears repeatedly into the hole.

Dances are performed for many reasons and in many ways around the world. However, dance has an equally important place in all cultures, as a way of keeping alive traditional beliefs, ideas and customs, and will continue to do so for centuries to come.

Siva dancing

Hand movements are very important in the Siva dance of Samoa. You can perform the dance either on your own or with friends, standing in a row.

1. Bend your knees. Tilt your head slightly to one side.

2. Move sideways, by firstly moving both your heels to the right, then sliding your toes to the right. Keep repeating this movement.

3. Move your hands in a circular motion, weaving patterns in the air.

▲ Many Pacific dances, such as this one in Tonga, use hand movements for expression and for story-telling.

Think of a story you would like to tell, and use your hands to describe it.

Glossary

Ancestors The people from whom a family is descended.

Ash Wednesday The first day of the Christian festival of Lent. It is called Ash Wednesday because of the custom of sprinkling ashes on the heads of worshippers on that day.

Authorities The governing powers within a society.

Birthright The rights and privileges that a person is believed to have as soon as he or she is born, usually determined by a society's customs and traditions.

Bugle A military instrument made of brass or copper. It is similar to a trumpet, but slightly smaller.

Cantonese A Chinese language originally from Canton, in southern China.

Cascade A constant flow.

Charcoal A black substance used for drawing and decoration, obtained from partly burnt wood or bone.

Chinese New Year The festival celebrating the New Year according to the Chinese calendar. It normally occurs in February.

Colonial A word which describes anything to do with a colony – a territory ruled by people from another place or country.

Crescent A half-moon shape.

Dock labourer A person who works in a shipyard.

Dreamtime According to Australian Aboriginal beliefs, Dreamtime was the period when the world was first created.

Elders The respected older members of a clan or community.

Emigrate To leave your own country and settle in a new one.

Fertility The ability to reproduce, or to produce fruit or crops in great quantities.

Fiesta The Spanish word for a festival or celebration.

Flamboyant Lively, colourful and entertaining.

Frenzied Wildly enthusiastic and active.

Gestures Specific movements of the body, used to express feelings or emotions.

Harvest The time of year when ripe crops are gathered in.

Hoarse When a voice sounds rough or deep, as if the speaker has a sore throat.

Jig A lively, springy dance.

Lent A period of forty days between Ash Wednesday and Easter, when Christians go without favourite foods or special things, in memory of Jesus Christ.

Mardi Gras The celebrations in New Orleans, USA, on Shrove Tuesday.

Maypole A high pole, often decorated with flowers, which people dance around in celebration of May Day (1 May).

Medicine man A person who heals the sick.

Meshed Tangled up.

Migrate To move in large numbers from one part of the world to another.

Military drill When soldiers parade and do exercises in time with each other, following shouted orders.

Mission school A school set up by Christian missionaries, which puts emphasis on religious teaching.

Mocking Making fun of somebody by imitating his or her speech or actions.

Ostrich The largest bird in the world, from the deserts of Africa and the Middle East.

Plantation An estate or farm, usually in a hot or tropical country, where crops are grown.

Plume A large, ornamental bird's feather.

Possessed Occupied or controlled by something, often a supernatural being or god.

Prosperity Having a lot of money, fortune or success.
Rank A person's official position within a society or organization.
Regiment A number of soldiers organized into a group.
Saint's day A specific date when a saint is honoured, usually his or her birthday.
Shaman A priest or healer who may use magic and rituals to heal people and to communicate with the spirits.
Sorcery The use of magic.
Trance A strange feeling, like being in a dream. People in a trance can often do daring or dangerous things without harming themselves.
Voodoo A religion that originated in Africa and is now practised in the Caribbean, the southern USA and parts of Brazil.

Books to read

Carnival Time, Armet Francis (Seed Publications, 1990)
Passport series (Franklin Watts)
My Belief series (Frankin Watts)
The Usborne Guide to Dance, L. Smith (Usborne, 1988)
Countries of the World series (Wayland)
Threatened Cultures series (Wayland)
People and Places series (Wayland)
Seasonal Festivals series (Wayland)

Index

The dance traditions in this book come from many different peoples. Various styles of dance are listed in the index, such as 'chain dances', 'fertility dances' and 'square dances'. If you want to see how dances are used, look at entries such as 'contests' and 'festivals'. You can use the 'peoples' entry to look up dances from the cultures mentioned in this book.